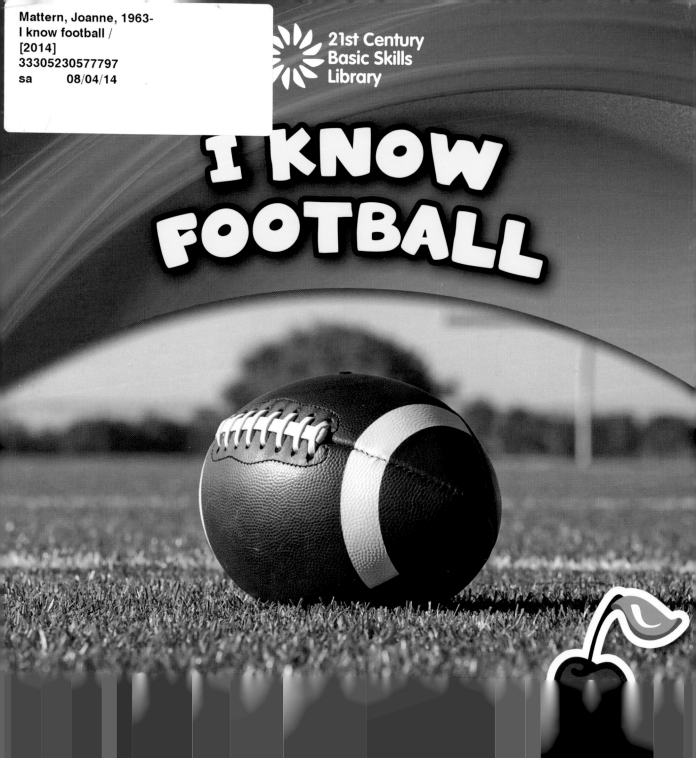

21st Century
Basic Skills
Library

I KNOW
FOOTBALL

Published in the United States of America
by Cherry Lake Publishing
Ann Arbor, Michigan
www.cherrylakepublishing.com

Consultant: Marla Conn, Read-Ability

Photo Credits: iStockphoto/Thinkstock, cover, 1; Library of Congress, 4; AP Images, 6; David Stluka/AP Images, 8; Richard Paul Kane/Shutterstock, 10, 12, 20; Mike Flippo/Shutterstock, 14; Aspen Photo/Shutterstock, 16; David Lee/Shutterstock, 18

Library of Congress Cataloging-in-Publication Data
Mattern, Joanne, 1963-
  I know football / Joanne Mattern.
    pages cm. -- (I know sports)
  ISBN 978-1-62431-399-8 (hardcover) -- ISBN 978-1-62431-475-9 (pbk.) -- ISBN 978-1-62431-437-7 (pdf) -- ISBN 978-1-62431-513-8 (ebook)
  1. Football--Juvenile literature. I. Title.
  GV950.7.M28 2013
  796.332--dc23
                                              2013006123

Cherry Lake Publishing would like to acknowledge the work of The Partnership for 21st Century Skills. Please visit *www.p21.org* for more information.

Printed in the United States of America
Corporate Graphics Inc.
July 2013
CLFA11

TABLE OF CONTENTS

History

Football is more than 100 years old. At first players only ran with the football. Later they passed the ball too.

The National Football League (NFL) began in 1920. It had 14 teams. Now the NFL has 32 teams.

The Super Bowl is the **championship** for the NFL. It takes place once a year. The first Super Bowl was played in 1967.

Equipment

Football is a tough sport. Players wear special **equipment** to stay safe.

Football players wear helmets. The helmets are hard plastic with cushions inside. The first helmets were made of leather.

Football players wear many pads. The pads keep players safe when they **tackle** or get hit.

Scoring

Each team tries to bring
the ball into the end zone.
This is scoring a **touchdown**.
A touchdown is worth
six points.

The team gets to try to score again after a touchdown. They usually try to kick the ball through the goal posts. This is one extra point.

A team can also kick a **field goal**. This is three points. The team with the most points at the end of the game wins.

Find Out More

BOOK

Wyatt, James. *Football*. New York: Gareth Stevens, 2012.

WEB SITE

NFL Rush

www.nflrush.com

The NFL Web site for kids has games, contests, and information on youth football.

Glossary

championship (CHAM-pee-uhn-ship) a game that decides which team wins a league title

equipment (i-KWIP-muhnt) objects used to play a game

field goal (FEELD GOHL) when a football is kicked through the goal posts to earn three points

tackle (TAK-uhl) to grab and bring a player to the ground

touchdown (TUHCH-doun) when a football is brought into the end zone to earn six points

Home and School Connection

Use this list of words from the book to help your child become a better reader. Word games and writing activities can help beginning readers reinforce literacy skills.

began	hit	passed	takes
cushions	kick	players	teams
each	league	point	through
end	made	ran	touchdown
equipment	more	safe	tough
first	most	score	try
football	now	special	wear
goal	old	sport	wins
has	only	super	years
helmets	pads	tackle	zone

Index

About the Author

Joanne Mattern loves all sports. Her husband helped her learn about football. Since then she has written biographies of many football players. Joanne lives with her family in New York State.